The Keepinnit Reels 3: Revenge Or Return Of The Snark

Michael Pollick

Published by Michael Pollick, 2024.

THE KEEPINNIT REELS 3: REVENGE OR RETURN OF THE SNARK

First edition. September 21, 2024.

ISBN: 979-8227920157

Written by Michael Pollick.

Table of Contents

The Keepinnit Reels 3: Revenge or Return of the Snark

Michael Pollick

A Sea Of Chocolate Milks: Lunchroom Monitor Confidential

Serving the public good on the grade school Student Council was a perk limited to two fortunate students per classroom. The chosen few manned the bookstore in the mornings, helped in the central office, or, in my case, became lunchroom monitors. As a sixth grader, this meant being the only Gulliver in a gymnasium filled with first-grade Lilliputs. I accepted the challenge.

Most of the time, the job involved crowd control, with the occasional Shell Answer Man moments thrown in. We politely but firmly pointed out where the lunch-packing sheep could graze, and made sure they returned their trays to the proper hair-netted authorities. However, there was one situation that took up almost all of our time, and it only cost a nickel. Milk cartons.

Opening a chocolate milk carton at age six required motor skills usually reserved for age seven or above. The milks would hit the tables and immediately a sea of hands shot up. Monitors dutifully went from child to child, bending and unfolding every carton. Once in a while, we had a rogue "me do it myself", but it only took one launch failure to bring him back to the fold. These kids today.

Petting Zoos: Can We Finally Stop Calling Them Fun?

Petting zoos were always on the short list of budget-friendly things to do on a 1970s Saturday, along with matinee movies, skating rinks, mall crawling, and bowling. However, the petting zoo was the only option that could end with fecal matter and gauze bandages. The main takeaway from petting zoos was that really smelly animals can have bad days, too.

Petting zoos sounded so good on paper. We'd get to spend quality time with domesticated farm animals, and they wouldn't have to produce eggs, milk, or meat for a while. Win, win. But petting zoo residents weren't the usual breed of goat or sheep. Endless hours of unsolicited petting had left them bitter and cynical. We weren't children to them, we were dried corn delivery systems. Never let them see the cup.

I don't blame the captives at a petting zoo for taking the occasional ounce of flesh or chewing a random piece of clothing. They didn't ask for this assignment, and I would probably do the same thing if I were in their position. I would hope the vending machines were filled with slices of pizza, though. Go ahead and pet me, kid, I've got nothing but time

The Hat Trick of Cool: MAGNUS Chord Organ, Clarinet, Accordion

Before synthesizers named Korg or Yamaha took the stage, there was the wheezy, breezy home version called a MAGNUS chord organ. An electric motor blew life into the machine as young instrumentalists plunked out public domain songs like "After The Ball" and "The Man Who Broke The Bank At Monte Carlo". The keys were numbered for our playing convenience, and the tone was positively asthmatic.

The next logical progression was the clarinet, beginning with rudimentary fourth-grade music lessons. You would think the first tune would be the timeless "Mary Had A Little Lamb", but before you can sail, you must learn to "Lightly Row". I spent a few years trying to master the swizzle stick, but rented instruments had a shelf life. I did manage to transition from the paint-by-number school to actual sight-reading, so it wasn't a total loss.

In Ohio during the '70s, if you didn't have an accordion, the state issued one. A Pentecostal minister loaned me his accordion so I could play in the church orchestra. We learned all of the songs in the hymnal, plus dozens of contemporary choruses and special music. Today, I'm the organist for a small Methodist church. I still haven't broken the bank at Monte Carlo, however.

Three Million Years Of Evil: Emus Make Lousy Housepets

For those who don't know, an emu is a flightless bird ostensibly native to Australia, but I personally think that's a cover story. In the '90s, emu farms became a cottage industry in the States, with the selling point of profitable meat, leather, feathers, and oil. Would-be farmers only had to keep a few dozen of these in the back forty and reap the benefits. The only part of the emu that survived the decade was its attitude. People were left with flocks of VERY angry birds.

So I'm visiting my mother-in-law at a rehabilitation center in rural Alabama, and I discovered a wildlife sanctuary of sorts next to the facility. There were wild turkeys, a few goats, pigs, and a pair of emu bullies from the wrong side of the pen. It was clear they controlled all of the food action, gobbling up anything we tossed over the fence. I had a pack of peanut butter crackers in my hand, and one of them noticed.

For a brief moment, I made eye contact and saw three million years of evil behind those red eyes. The next few seconds were a blur as the emu's beak made contact, broke my grip, and snagged the crackers. As I nursed my hand and admitted to my wife she was right all along, my thoughts turned to meat, leather, feathers, and oil.

Eight-Track Tapes: NOT The Cutting Edge of '70s Technology

If you truly wanted Frampton to come alive in your brother's 1974 El Camino, you were going to do it through the courtesy of an eight-track tape player. Vinyl records may have been great on the portable hi-fi, but not in a moving vehicle. Eight-track tapes were designed specifically to take whatever abuse you could dish out, and conveniently fit in a gorilla-approved Samsonite suitcase.

The main problem with eight-track tapes could be summed up in one nonsense word: KERCHUNK. Unlike vinyl albums, eight-tracks featured four channels that were not necessarily synched with the songs. When it was time to switch channels, Robert Plant would just stop singing about hedgerows, there would be a loud kerchunk, and dead air for at least 30 seconds before he'd buy that stairway. Meanwhile, you could hear all of the other tracks playing in reverse, like testimony in a backward masking trial.

A total lack of navigation also brought down the eight-track tape. If you wanted to boogie down to Disco Inferno, you'd have to punch through every channel until you got somewhere in the neighborhood. There was no fast forward or reverse, and if the tape lasted longer than the album, channel 4 featured 20 minutes of pure nothing. Welcome to our nightmare.

Keeping The "Square" In Square Dancing:
Bow To The Inevitable

Gym teachers in Ohio were often inspired by quaint local traditions, so for sixth graders, this meant the well-known aerobic exercise called square dancing. When we weren't hurling fireballs or firing floor hockey pucks, we were bowing to our corners and promenading back home. Any outside observer would notice instantly that NONE of us wanted to be in our skins at that moment. We only did what the nice recording told us to do.

It's important to keep in mind that this was taking place squarely during the Disco era. While other kids were moving and grooving to Elton John, Rod Stewart or Donna Summer, we were busy twisting ourselves into convoluted poses while fiddles and banjos sawed away. If the gym teacher actually had his pulse on the Cleveland-area scene, we would have been learning how to do the polka and the Chicken Dance instead.

Fortunately, the middle school gym teachers took pity on us and taught us modern line dances like the Electric Slide, the Hustle, and the Continental. No more corners, no more partners, just a line of 13-year-olds getting down with our bad selves. Twenty-year high school reunions, here we come!

Yes
PIZZIARIAS
Yes
Yes
COOKIES
APLE NUT
GOOEYS'

Yes Yes Cookies, Pizzarias, And Maple Nut Goodies: Gimme Back My Snack Bullets

One of my first food memories involved a coconut and caramel-based treat my neighbor called a "Yes Yes cookie". It covered all the bases as far as I was concerned– sweet, crunchy, bite-sized, and available. The other cookies on the shelves were okay, but the Yes Yes cookies took me to Flavor Town. A few years down the road, however, there were no more Yes Yes cookies to be found. In fact, many people accused me of making the whole thing up. They weren't always wrong.

A more savory snack showed up in the 80s, flour-based chips called Pizzarias. Pizzarias had an intoxicating blend of Italian spices and a powdered tomato seasoning. These chips hit differently than the usual corn-based chips we usually got. Pizza-flavored anything was already a rare treat, so these became my default setting. Once again, the powers-that-be decided to take a beautiful snack away from me.

The last to go was a complicated candy called Maple Nut Goodies. There were ground peanuts mixed with caramel, with a maple-flavored shell. They usually hung out at the candy island in department stores. I could usually find a bagged version at a dollar store, but no more. In a world of Circus Peanuts and Candy Corn, I want to be a Screaming Yellow Zonker.

Driver's Ed Teachers: Nerves Of Steel, Buckets Of Sweat

In Ohio during the '80s, there were only three ways someone under 18 could legally get their driver's license. The first way was to actually turn 18, which gave you the right to enter any examination center and schedule a driving test. For a lot of us 16-year-olds, however, this was a frustrating example of delayed gratification. We wanted to drive to the mall, and we wanted to drive NOW. A mere permit wasn't going to cut it anymore.

The second option was to enroll in what we half-jokingly called a "crash course". For a fee, local stores such as Sears or Montgomery Ward offered four-day driving classes, with the carrot of a required certificate at the end. The local insult hurled at any driver who committed an act of stupidity became "WHERE DID YOU LEARN TO DRIVE? SEARS?" It got the job done, but at what cost?

Finally, there was the more affordable 18-week driver's ed course in high school. My instructor was an avid cyclist, and he would remind us daily that he was training us to drive on the same roads he used. He also called the permits "Death Certificates", and we weren't allowed to thank him. Considering how some of my own practice sessions went, I can't say I blame him.

Vice-Principals And Guidance Counselors: These Were ACTUAL Job Titles, Right?

The daily high school ritual started and ended with a cast of familiar characters. There was Fred, the perpetually exasperated bus driver. Agnes the hall monitor kept us at bay until the official bell rang. Of course, all of our teachers were in their assigned classrooms, not finishing a final smoke and coffee in the teacher's lounge or anything. A few of us even caught an occasional glimpse of Mister Johnson, the principal and founder of the educational feast.

As the day ground on, however, two upper management cast members stood out the most: The Vice-Principal and the Guidance Counselor. If the principal was responsible for the teachers' well-being and the parents' de-fanging, the vice-principal's main charge was student law enforcement. This was the original thankless job. He wasn't a heartbeat away from becoming principal, he was thousands of detentions away from earning his pension.

The guidance counselor was the other authority figure with whom we formed an uneasy alliance. His job description sounded straightforward on paper, but in reality the guidance counselor had to be all things to all people. Part psychologist, part Sorting Hat, and EVERY student club's faculty sponsor. Heavy was the head that could access every SAT score

Lays
Lays
Lays
Lays
Propps
Propps
Propps
Propps
Propps
Dooops
Propps
Propps
Propps
Kruppin
Noodles
Chato
Snaps
Cheezzy Whajea
Kruppin
Snaps
Krunchy
Knibles
Krunchy
Snipplo
Chato
Snaps
Chato
Snaps
Yoto
Snaps
Snap
Snaps

Crimes Against Humanity: Snack Aisle Edition

I realized snack food companies had lost their collective minds when I saw an endcap filled with bags of "Rooty Tooty, Fresh N Frooty"...potato chips. Somehow the idea of combining the unholy sweetness of a pancake breakfast and the savory saltiness of potato chips sounded like money in the bank to an entire Research and Development department. It made me wonder if all snack food producers have a random flavor generator in the back room. One spin and we get "Barbecue" "Lemon" "Corn" "Zonkers". Another spin, and it's all Rooty Tooty.

When did those snacking geniuses decide to Bogart the best flavors? I heard rumors of a Monterey Jack cheese-flavored Dorito, only to discover it's only offered in the more discriminating Stop-And-Robs or General Family Dollar Tree Deals stores. By the time I call in a favor at the Pentagon and get the coordinates, some undeserving customer gets the last bag.

My dream job now is to name all the trendy new snack foods. We'll see aisles filled with Cheezy Wheezies, Krunchy Kibbles, Flamin' Cheddar Jelly Jammers, and Noogie Nuggets. I just DARE Walmart not to add them to the roster.

The Agony and the Anger of High School Dodgeball

You know what I remember most about high school? Dodgeball. Yeah, that glorious game where you realize who your friends are and who will throw you under the bus—literally. I mean, it's like they took the concept of gym class and turned it into a gladiator arena. You walk in thinking, "I'm just here to get my gym credit," and suddenly, you're in a battle for your life!

First off, there's always that one kid, the human cannonball, who's just way too into it. You know the one—he's got the arm of a major league pitcher and the aim of a sniper. You're dodging left and right, trying to avoid becoming a human target, while he's just cackling like a villain from a cartoon. And let's not forget the strategy: it's all about forming alliances. You're scanning the court, thinking, "Okay, who's on my side? Who's just waiting to throw me to the wolves?"

Then there's the moment you catch the ball. Suddenly, you're a hero! You're like, "Yes! I've saved my friend!" But then you realize you've just put a target on your back. It's like winning a game of musical chairs but with more sweat and betrayal.

And let's be real, the real victory is surviving the post-game locker room. You're just trying to wash off the shame of being hit in the face, while everyone's laughing like it's a comedy show. Ah, dodgeball—where friendships are forged and shattered in the blink of an eye!

From Vest to Prime Time: The Unmasked Truth About Safety Patrol

You remember being on safety patrol in elementary school? Oh, the glory! It was like being given a badge of honor, but really, it was just a fluorescent vest that screamed, "I'm here to ruin your fun!" I mean, who knew that standing outside in the freezing cold, trying to look important while kids ignored you was a rite of passage?

There I was, strutting my stuff like I was the principal of the playground. "Stop running!" I'd shout, as if I had the power to freeze time. But let's be real, the only thing I was good at was getting ignored by kids who were way too busy perfecting their ninja moves. And don't even get me started on the traffic. I was basically a glorified traffic cone, waving my little sign like, "Hey, you! Yes, you! Don't hit the kids!"

And the meetings? Oh, the meetings! They were like secret society gatherings where we discussed the fine art of stopping kids from playing tag on the blacktop. "Remember, safety first!" they'd say, while we all nodded like we were in on some big secret.

But the best part? The power trips! I mean, I could tell the fifth graders to "slow down" and they'd look at me like I was the law! I felt like I was in a cop movie, just without the donuts. So here's to safety patrol—where we learned the true meaning of authority... and how to look fabulous in neon!

The Cat Whisperer and the Composting Queen: A Tale of Unlikely Encounters

So, I finally decided it was time to meet my neighbors. You know, the people I've been avoiding like they were the last slice of pizza at a party. I mean, who needs that kind of commitment? But curiosity got the best of me, and I thought, "How bad could it be?" Spoiler alert: very bad.

I knocked on the first door, and this guy answers, looking like he just rolled out of a 90s grunge band reunion. He's got a cat on his shoulder, and I'm pretty sure it was judging me harder than my high school English teacher. I introduced myself, and he just stared at me like I had three heads. Turns out, he's a "cat whisperer." I didn't know that was a thing! So, naturally, I had to ask if he could whisper a few things to my cat, who thinks I'm just a glorified food dispenser.

Next door, I met the woman who had a garden that looked like it belonged in a magazine. I complimented her on it, and she launched into a 20-minute monologue about composting. I didn't even know composting had a backstory! She was like a gardening TED Talk on steroids.

By the end of my "meet the neighbors" adventure, I felt like I'd signed up for a reality show. So now I'm back home, contemplating whether to invest in cat whispering lessons or start my own composting channel. Because honestly, if you can't beat 'em, join 'em, right?

The Battle for the Backyard: A Child's Quest to Conquer the Lawn

So, there I was, a kid with dreams bigger than my backyard, ready to conquer the wild jungle of grass that my parents called a lawn. They handed me the mower like it was Excalibur, and I felt like a knight about to slay a dragon. Spoiler alert: the dragon was just a bunch of dandelions, but I was determined to emerge victorious.

I fired up that mower, and let me tell you, it roared to life like a beast. I was ready to be the hero of my own action movie. But then, I realized I had no idea what I was doing. I gripped the handle like it was a steering wheel, and suddenly, I was in a high-speed chase—except the only thing I was chasing was my own sanity. I zigzagged across the lawn like I was trying to avoid an invisible minefield. I think I even mowed a perfect spiral at one point—totally unintentional, but hey, modern art, right?

And then, there was the moment of truth: the grass clippings. I had no clue what to do with them. I thought I was supposed to gather them up like trophies, but I ended up creating a grass confetti explosion that would make any party jealous. By the end of it, I was covered in more grass than the lawn itself. My parents came outside, and I stood there, a sweaty, grass-stained warrior, and they just laughed. I guess that's the real victory—making memories, even if they're a little messy.

Fossil Hunting Fiascos: A Childhood Full of Dirt, Disappointment, and Potatoes

You ever go fossil hunting as a kid? I mean, what a wild ride! Picture this: me, armed with a little plastic shovel and a bucket that couldn't hold more than a couple of rocks, convinced I was the next Indiana Jones. My mom was all in, saying, "Go find a dinosaur!" Like, okay, Mom, but I'm pretty sure they're not just hanging out in the backyard.

So, there I am, digging through the dirt like I'm on some grand archaeological expedition, but really, I'm just unearthing old dog bones and maybe a long-lost Lego piece. I once found this rock that looked suspiciously like a dinosaur egg. I was like, "Mom, I'm rich! I'm gonna be famous!" Turns out, it was just a really ugly potato.

And don't get me started on my friends! They'd show up with their fancy metal detectors and I'd be there with my bucket of "treasures," convinced I was about to discover a T-Rex skull. Instead, I found a rusty nail and a bottle cap. I mean, at least I could've made a cool art project, right?

But the best part? When I finally found a real fossil, I was so excited I dropped it, and it shattered into a million pieces. So much for my future in paleontology! But hey, at least I got a great story, a few scrapes, and a lifelong appreciation for rocks that look like potatoes. Fossil hunting: it's basically just glorified dirt digging!

The Ultimate Betrayal: The Truth About Raking Leaves as a Kid

You ever notice how raking leaves as a kid is basically the ultimate betrayal? Like, one minute you're jumping into piles of crunchy, colorful leaves, feeling like a woodland creature in a Disney movie, and the next, your parents hand you a rake like it's a sword and say, "Time to earn your keep!"

And let's talk about the rake. It's this giant, medieval torture device that seems designed specifically to ruin your day. You're out there, a tiny warrior battling the forces of nature, and the leaves? They're like, "Oh, you thought you got us all? Surprise! We're back!" It's a never-ending cycle of leaf warfare.

You start off all optimistic, right? You grab that rake, and for a glorious five minutes, you're a leaf-collecting machine. But then? Oh, the fatigue hits. Your arms are screaming, and you're pretty sure you've raked up the entire neighborhood's leaves. You look at your pile, and it's like, "Is this it? This is my life now?"

And then comes the moment of glory: you finally finish, you step back to admire your work, and what happens? A gust of wind swoops in like a villain and scatters your hard-earned pile everywhere! It's like the universe is saying, "Nice try, kiddo!"

So, you know what? I say embrace the chaos. Next time, I'm just going to grab a leaf blower, put on some sunglasses, and call it a day. Because honestly, who needs cardio when you've got leaf drama?

Dodging Dogs and Banking Change: The Invaluable Skillset of a Paperboy

You know, back in the day, when kids had real jobs—like, you know, delivering newspapers? Yeah, that was me, your friendly neighborhood paperboy. I was like a pint-sized superhero, except my cape was a backpack full of newspapers, and my superpower was dodging angry dogs. Seriously, every morning was an obstacle course. I'd wake up at the crack of dawn, looking like a zombie, dragging myself out of bed, and my mom would be like, "You're going to be late!" And I'm like, "Mom, it's 5 AM! The sun isn't even awake yet!"

So, I grab my stack of newspapers, which, by the way, weighed more than I did, and hit the streets. First house, I'm feeling like a boss, tossing that paper like I'm in the MLB. Second house, I miss the porch completely, and it lands in the flowerbed. Sorry, Mrs. Johnson! Your begonias are getting a special delivery today!

Then there were the dogs. Oh, the dogs! I swear, it was like I was running a marathon, dodging these furry beasts. One time, I swear I saw a Rottweiler eyeing me like I was a walking steak. I took off like I was in the Olympics, and I'm pretty sure I set a record for the fastest paper route in history.

But you know what? I wouldn't trade those mornings for anything. I learned to hustle, dodge danger, and perfect my paper-tossing skills. And hey, I got to keep the change! So, yeah, paper routes were basically my first taste of entrepreneurship.

From Evel Knievel to Embarrassment: A Cautionary Tale of Backyard Stunting

You ever notice how backyard stunts seem like a great idea until you actually try them? I mean, there I was, feeling like a cross between Evel Knievel and a kid who just discovered sugar. I grabbed my bike, which is basically a glorified hunk of metal with wheels, and thought, "Today's the day I become a legend." Spoiler alert: I did not become a legend.

So, I set up my "ramp," which was really just a couple of old crates stacked on top of each other. Safety gear? Pfft, who needs that? I'm invincible! I pedaled back, heart racing, adrenaline pumping, and launched off that ramp like a majestic eagle—if that eagle was also a clumsy toddler. I soared for approximately two seconds before gravity kicked in, and suddenly, I was a human cannonball headed for the ground.

The landing? Let's just say my backyard is now a monument to my poor decision-making skills. I hit the ground, and my bike flipped over like it was auditioning for a circus act. My neighbor's cat watched me with this judgmental stare, like, "Really? You thought that was going to work?"

Now, I'm nursing a bruised ego and a sore backside, but hey, at least I have a new TikTok video to post! Who needs a career in stunts when you can have a viral moment that makes everyone laugh? So, remember folks, if you're going to stunt, maybe invest in some pads—or at least a better ramp!

The Thrill of the Hunt: Nostalgic Flea Market Adventures

You ever been to a flea market as a kid? It's like stepping into a treasure hunt, but instead of gold doubloons, you're digging through a mountain of questionable antiques and mystery boxes that might contain a rare Beanie Baby or just a sock. My mom would drag me along, and I'd be like, "Great, another day of sifting through grandma's attic."

First, there's the smell. You know that smell? It's a mix of fried food, musty old books, and the lingering scent of desperation. You walk in and immediately question your life choices. But then, you see it—a table piled high with toys, and suddenly you're Indiana Jones, dodging booby traps of old VHS tapes and ceramic cats.

And let's talk about the vendors. They're like characters in a sitcom. There's the one who's convinced that every piece of junk is a rare artifact. "This is a vintage 1970s toaster!" No, Bob, it's a toaster that probably burned down someone's kitchen. And then there's the lady with the homemade jewelry made from bottle caps. I'm not saying it's ugly, but I'm pretty sure I saw her wearing the same stuff when I was five.

But the best part? Haggling! As a kid, I thought I was a master negotiator. "I'll give you a dollar for this dinosaur toy." And they'd look at me like I just offered them a penny for their thoughts. Ah, the flea market—where dreams and bizarre trinkets collide, and every trip feels like an episode of "What Not to Buy."

A Blast from the Past: Revisiting the Ridiculousness of High School Football

So, I went to a high school football game the other night, and let me tell you, it was like stepping into a time machine back to my teenage years, except this time I was armed with an adult's understanding of how utterly ridiculous all of it is. First off, the parking lot! It's like a scene from a reality show—parents tailgating like they're prepping for the Super Bowl, while teenagers are busy trying to look cool in their oversized hoodies. I mean, who knew high school football was the Olympics of social status?

Then there's the concession stand, where the prices are basically a second mortgage. Seriously, I paid $8 for a lukewarm hot dog that could double as a doorstop. And don't even get me started on the nachos! It's like they took a bag of chips and said, "Let's drown these in cheese sauce and hope for the best."

As I settled into my seat, I realized I was surrounded by the same cliques I remember: the cheerleaders, the band kids, and the guys who think wearing a jersey makes them a pro athlete. And the halftime show? Oh boy! It was like watching a live episode of "America's Got Talent," but with fewer talents and more awkward dance moves.

By the end of the night, I was just grateful for the nostalgia, the laughter, and the realization that some things never change—like the thrill of watching a bunch of teenagers chase a ball under the Friday night lights.

Pizza
FREE

Pizza Hut's Cheesy Salvation: A Journey Through the 80s

So, let me take you back to the 1980s, a time when Pizza Hut was basically the pinnacle of fine dining. I mean, if you were a kid, nothing screamed "special occasion" like a trip to that red-roofed haven of cheese and carbs. You walk in, and it's like entering a culinary time machine. The smell of pepperoni and nostalgia hits you like a warm hug from your grandma.

You're greeted by those iconic checkered tables, and you know it's about to get real. You sit down, and there it is—an all-you-can-eat buffet! I'm talking about a pizza smorgasbord that would make even the most disciplined dieter weep. You could pile your plate high with slices, and nobody judged you. It was like a buffet for your soul!

Now, let's talk about the salad bar—a green oasis in a sea of carbs. You'd load up on croutons like they were gold nuggets, slathering ranch dressing like it was a life or death situation. And don't even get me started on the dessert pizza! Who thought "let's put frosting on pizza" was a good idea? I mean, it sounds ridiculous, but in the 80s, that was basically gourmet cuisine.

And as you're devouring your fifth slice, your parents are just sitting there, sipping on their Pepsi, thinking they're living the high life. Honestly, if you weren't eating at Pizza Hut, were you even eating? It was the place where dreams were made, one cheesy slice at a time!

A Magical Land of Reel Wonder: Remembering the Joy of Video Store Visits

Remember the thrill of going to a video rental store as a kid? It was like stepping into a candy shop, but instead of sweets, it was all about VHS tapes and that distinct smell of popcorn and regret. You'd walk in, and it was like entering a magical land where the latest blockbuster was just waiting for you, assuming you could dodge the angry parents who were definitely not here for the 27th consecutive week of "The Lion King."

I'd grab that little plastic card, feeling like a VIP, only to realize I'd forgotten my mom's credit card, which was basically the golden ticket. So there I was, standing in front of the shelves, trying to look cool while my heart raced. I mean, how do you choose between "Titanic" and "Space Jam"? One's a love story that made everyone cry, and the other had Michael Jordan and cartoons!

And don't even get me started on the covers. You'd pick one up, and the artwork was so epic, you thought, "This has to be good!" Spoiler alert: it usually wasn't. Then, there was the pressure of the checkout line. You'd hear the beeps of the scanner and pray it wouldn't beep for that one tape you accidentally dropped in the candy aisle.

Finally, you'd leave with your prized possession, feeling like you conquered the world. Then, three days later, you'd be back, staring at the same shelves, ready for another adventure. Ah, the nostalgia!

Cheesy Chaos: When a Simple Sandwich Goes Horribly Wrong

So, I decided to make a grilled cheese sandwich for the first time. I mean, how hard could it be? It's just bread and cheese, right? I'm practically a culinary genius! I grab my bread, and I'm feeling like Gordon Ramsay, but then I realize I don't even know what kind of cheese to use. Is American cheese the only option? I feel like I'm about to start a cheese war.

I settle on two slices of the most questionable cheese I could find in my fridge. I mean, it's cheese, it's gotta work. I butter the bread like I'm painting a masterpiece, and I'm already picturing my future TikTok fame. I throw it in the pan and immediately panic because it's sizzling like it's auditioning for a cooking show.

Five seconds in, I'm already regretting my life choices. I flip it too soon, and it's a disaster! Half the cheese is stuck to the pan, and the other half is trying to escape. I'm wrestling with this sandwich like it's my long-lost rival.

Finally, I plate it and take a bite. It's... well, it's a grilled cheese, but it's also a reminder that I should probably stick to takeout. I mean, who knew that making a sandwich could feel like a scene from a horror movie? But hey, at least I can say I tried! And now I'm officially qualified to judge all your grilled cheese skills from the comfort of my couch.

The Illusion of Wealth: A Childhood Perspective

You remember getting an allowance as a kid? Oh, the thrill of it! My parents handed me a crisp five-dollar bill every week like it was a golden ticket to Willy Wonka's factory. I'd strut around like I was a millionaire, ready to conquer the world. Five bucks! I was practically Elon Musk in my mind. But let's be real, that five dollars could buy me a pack of gum, maybe a candy bar... if I was feeling wild, a soda. I was living large!

But my allowance came with rules. You know, the classic "you have to do chores" deal. I was like, "Chores? For five bucks? I could have just mowed the neighbor's lawn and made twenty!" But no, I was stuck folding laundry and washing dishes, which, let's be honest, didn't even pay in snacks.

And the best part? My parents would sit me down for "financial advice." "Save your money, invest it wisely," they'd say, while I was just trying to figure out if I could afford a new toy or if I had to wait another week. So, I'd save up, and guess what? I'd end up spending it all on the dumbest things! Like that glow-in-the-dark slime that promised to change my life but ended up ruining my carpet.

In the end, I learned two things: money doesn't buy happiness, but it sure buys a lot of candy, and chores are just a fancy way of saying, "We're not paying you enough for this."

MEN
WOMEN

The Art of Swift Retreat: A Bathroom Entrance Gone Wrong

So, picture this: I'm at this fancy coffee shop, right? I've got my latte, my laptop, and an urgent call of nature. I strut confidently to the restroom, thinking, "I've got this." I push open the door and—oh boy, what a surprise! I'm suddenly in a room that looks like a Pinterest board exploded.

I mean, there are plants everywhere, and I swear I saw a sign that said, "Welcome to the Goddess Den." I'm standing there, frozen, like I just walked into the wrong dimension. I quickly glance around, and it hits me: I've entered the women's restroom. Panic sets in. I start to backtrack, but then I hear the unmistakable sound of a toilet flushing. Oh no, too late!

Now, I'm committed. I can't just turn around—what if someone sees? So, I shuffle in like I'm trying to blend in at a yoga retreat, praying nobody notices me. I'm half-expecting someone to ask if I'm here for the "Sisterhood of the Traveling Pants" meeting.

And then it happens. A woman walks in, looks at me, and I can see the wheels turning in her head. I'm just standing there, desperately trying to look like I belong, like, "Yes, I too enjoy floral scents and soft lighting."

Finally, I bolt out, my dignity trailing behind me like a bad haircut. Moral of the story? Always check the signs. Because let's be honest, the only thing worse than walking into the wrong restroom is walking out of it!

HIGH SCORES

Leveling Up: An Odyssey to the Top of the Arcade

So, picture this: it's a Saturday afternoon, and I'm at the arcade, which, let's be real, is basically my second home. I'm surrounded by flashing lights, the sound of coins clinking, and the smell of stale popcorn. There's this game, "Galactic Invaders," and I've been eyeing the high score board like it's the final rose ceremony on a reality show.

Now, the reigning champ, "DudeBro89," has a score that's basically a phone number. I mean, who has that much time? But today, I'm feeling lucky. I pop in my quarters, and it's game on. I'm dodging pixels like I'm in a dance-off with a glitchy robot. I'm sweating, I'm shaking, and I'm pretty sure my heart rate is doing the Macarena.

As I get closer to that high score, I start to zone out everything around me. The world fades away. I'm not just a player; I'm a hero on a quest! Finally, I hit the final boss, and my fingers are flying over those buttons like I'm trying to summon a spell. And then... BOOM! I beat it. I beat the high score!

I'm screaming, "I'm the champion!" while everyone stares at me like I just won an Olympic medal. I take a selfie with the screen, and in that moment, I'm not just a gamer; I'm a legend. And then I realize—I forgot to save my name. Thanks, "DudeBro89." Your reign is safe for now!

The Ultimate Teenage Disaster: When Asking a Girl Out Goes Horribly Wrong

So, picture this: I'm fourteen, the age when your heart races at the thought of holding hands and your brain is a chaotic mess of hormones and awkwardness. I had a crush on this girl, let's call her Sarah. She was the kind of girl who could make a potato sack look like a runway outfit. One day, I decided it was time to ask her out. I mean, how hard could it be? Spoiler alert: very hard.

I spent the whole day rehearsing in front of the mirror, practicing my smoothest lines. "Hey, Sarah, wanna go get ice cream?" Easy, right? But as the school bell rang, my confidence evaporated faster than my mom's attempts at cooking. I approached her, and my brain was like, "Run! You're about to embarrass yourself!" But I pushed through, heart pounding like I was about to fight a bear.

I finally blurted out, "So, um, do you want to... uh... go out?" And I swear, time froze. She looked at me like I'd just asked her to join a cult. Her response? "Go out where?" I panicked and said, "To... um... get ice cream?" She burst out laughing, and I felt my face turn fifty shades of red.

In that moment, I realized I'd just invited her to a date in the most awkward way possible. She said yes, but only because she thought it would be funny. And that, my friends, is how I learned that rejection is just a punchline waiting to happen!

The Razor's Edge: A 13-Year-Old's Journey into the Unknown

So, picture this: I'm thirteen, full of bravado, and convinced I'm about to unlock the secrets of manhood by doing something I've seen in movies a million times—shaving. I sneak into the bathroom like a ninja, armed with my dad's razor, which, by the way, looks like it's seen more action than a superhero in a blockbuster.

I'm staring at my reflection, thinking, "How hard can this be?" Spoiler alert: very hard. My face is a barren wasteland, but I've got a couple of awkward peach fuzz hairs that I'm determined to conquer. I lather up with shaving cream, which, let's be honest, looks more like a marshmallow explosion than anything useful.

I take a deep breath, channel my inner barber, and start gliding the razor across my face like I'm painting the Mona Lisa. Except it's not art; it's chaos. I'm pretty sure I just gave myself a mini road map of nicks and cuts. By the time I'm done, I look less like a suave gentleman and more like I just lost a fight with a cheese grater.

And the best part? I walk out of the bathroom, proudly showing off my "shaved" face, only for my dad to burst out laughing. "You know that's not how it works, right?" Thanks, Dad, for the vote of confidence. So, if you're a teenager thinking about shaving for the first time, just remember: it's not a rite of passage; it's a rite of bloodshed!

From "The REAL Dog Owner's Survival Guide"

The Struggle is Real: Navigating Life with a Big Dog and a Small Lap

I never thought I'd find myself in this situation, but here I am, a proud owner of a Great Dane who believes he's a lap dog. I mean, I get it. He's got the heart of a puppy, the energy of a tornado, and the charm of a stand-up comedian. But the reality is, when you're a dog that weighs more than some small children, the idea of being a lap dog is a bit of a stretch—literally and figuratively.

It all started when I brought him home. I thought, "What a sweet, gentle giant!" He looked up at me with those big, soulful eyes, and I was convinced he'd be the perfect companion. Little did I know, the moment I sat down on the couch, my life would change forever. There he was, bounding over like a freight train, tail wagging like a propeller, and before I could even brace myself, he plopped down right on my lap. I swear, I heard my knees creak in protest.

Now, let's talk about the physics of this situation. A Great Dane is not meant to be a lap dog. They're built like a small horse, and here I was, trying to maintain my dignity while my new best friend treated me like a beanbag chair. I couldn't breathe, I couldn't move, and I definitely couldn't change the channel. I thought I might have to call for backup, but who do you even call in a situation like this? The canine equivalent of a bouncer? "Excuse me, could you please remove this 150-pound furball from my lap? He's crushing my dreams of ever being comfortable again."

At first, I tried to be patient. I'd gently push him off and say, "Buddy, you're too big for this!" But he'd just tilt his head, looking at me with that innocent expression as if to say, "What? I'm just trying to love you." And how could I argue with that? So, I'd relent, and he'd settle back down, taking up residence like he owned the place. I started to wonder if I'd accidentally adopted a dog or a small mountain.

Friends would come over, and they'd laugh, pointing out the absurdity of the situation. "Is that your dog or your new coffee table?" they'd joke. I'd roll my eyes, but deep down, I knew they had a point. It was a circus act every time I had guests. I'd offer them a seat, and they'd look at my dog, then at me, and back at my dog, weighing their options. "I'll just stand, thanks," they'd say, clearly not wanting to risk life and limb by sitting next to a dog that could crush them like a soda can.

Then there were the moments when he'd try to curl up. Picture this: a massive dog trying to curl into a ball on my lap, his legs sticking out at odd angles, his head hanging off the side of the couch like a sad, oversized ornament. I couldn't help but laugh. "You're not a cat, buddy!" I'd chuckle, but he'd just look at me, completely unfazed, as if he was the most elegant creature in the room.

I've learned to embrace the chaos. I've invested in a sturdy couch, a good chiropractor, and a sense of humor that could rival a stand-up comedian. My life has turned into a series of hilarious moments, like trying to sneak snacks while he's draped across my lap, or attempting to get up for a bathroom break without waking the sleeping giant.

In the end, I wouldn't trade it for anything. Sure, my lap is no longer my own, and my couch has seen better days, but the love and laughter that come with having a Great Dane who thinks he's a lap dog are worth every squished moment. After all, who needs personal space when you have a furry friend who thinks you're the best thing since squeaky toys?

When Your Dog's Stare Speaks Louder Than Words

You know, there's something about the way a dog looks at you that can pierce right through your soul. I mean, we're talking about a level of intensity that rivals any staring contest you've ever had with a human. It's like they've been trained in the art of eye contact by some ancient order of canine monks. You're just sitting there, minding your own business, and suddenly, your dog locks eyes with you. It's not just a casual glance; it's a full-on, laser-focused gaze that says, "I see you, human, and I'm judging you."

At first, it's cute, right? You're thinking, "Aww, look at my little furball! So affectionate!" But then, as the seconds tick by, you start to feel the pressure. It's like your dog is trying to read your mind or maybe even your soul. "Are you thinking about dinner? Because I'm thinking about dinner. You're not going to forget to feed me, are you?" And there it is—the judgment. You can almost hear them thinking, "If you don't get up and feed me right now, I will unleash the full power of my cuteness on you."

I swear, there's a point where that innocent stare transforms into something far more sinister. You know that moment when your dog's eyes widen just a fraction more? It's like they're channeling their inner philosopher, contemplating the meaning of life while simultaneously plotting your demise if you don't produce a treat within the next five seconds. And suddenly, you're not just a pet owner; you're a servant, a mere mortal at the mercy of this fluffy deity who demands snacks and belly rubs like they're the most sacred offerings known to dogkind.

And then there's the drool. Oh, the drool. Your dog's intense gaze is often accompanied by that slow, dramatic drool that hangs precariously from their jowls, threatening to fall at any moment. It's almost like they're trying to distract you with their sheer adorableness while simultaneously reminding you of their primal hunger. "Look into my eyes, human. Ignore the drool. Focus on my needs." You can't help but laugh at the absurdity of it all. Here you are, a grown adult, reduced to a state of utter servitude by a creature that thinks a squirrel is the most fascinating thing on the planet.

And let's not forget the moments when you're just trying to relax. You plop down on the couch, ready to binge-watch your favorite show, and there's your dog, sitting right in front of you, staring like you've just committed the ultimate betrayal. "What do you mean you're not paying attention to me? I'm right here!" It's as if they think your undivided attention is their birthright. You could have a PhD in psychology, but in the eyes of your dog, you're just a lowly servant who has failed to prioritize their needs.

Sometimes, I wonder if they're secretly judging our life choices. "Really? That's the show you're watching? You could be taking me for a walk, but instead, you're watching people get kicked off a reality show? What a waste of time." The intensity of their gaze seems to say, "You could be living your best life, but here you are, glued to the couch, while I could be chasing my own tail."

And there you are, caught in the crossfire of your dog's unwavering gaze, feeling both amused and slightly ashamed. You start to realize that maybe, just maybe, they're right. Maybe you should get up and take them for that walk. Because if you don't, who knows what kind of judgmental thoughts are swirling around in that furry little head? The next time your dog locks eyes with you, remember: it's not just a stare; it's a challenge, a plea, and a reminder that you're not the one in charge. You're simply living in their world, and they're just letting you know who really runs the show.

The Art of Negotiation: Why My Dog is the Best in the Kingdom

You know, I've always been told that dogs are man's best friend, but I think they might actually be the best negotiators in the animal kingdom. Take my dog, for instance. He's a golden retriever, a fluffy ball of sunshine with a tail that could power a small wind turbine. But when it comes to getting outside, he's like a seasoned politician, armed with a strategy that would put any PR team to shame.

It starts with the look. You know the one. Those big, soulful eyes that seem to say, "I haven't seen the great outdoors in at least five minutes, and I'm pretty sure I'm going to die of boredom if I don't get out there immediately." He'll plant himself right in front of me, his tail wagging like he's signaling an incoming flight. I swear, if his eyes could speak, they'd be saying, "Help me, human! The squirrels are plotting against me, and I need to investigate!"

Now, you might think that I'm heartless for ignoring this pleading gaze, but let me tell you, I've got my reasons. First of all, it's not like I can just drop everything and rush outside every time he decides he wants to sniff a blade of grass. I mean, I have responsibilities. There's laundry to fold, dishes to wash, and let's not forget the important business of scrolling through social media. But my dog? He doesn't care about my adulting duties. He's a creature of instinct, a furry embodiment of pure desire. And right now, that desire is to go outside.

So, after a few minutes of intense eye contact, he escalates his tactics. The whining starts. It's not just any whining; it's the kind that can pierce through the thickest wall of concentration. It's a sound that says, "I am suffering, human! My existence is a tragedy! Can't you see that I'm being held prisoner in this house?" At this point, I'm feeling a mix of guilt and annoyance. How can a creature so cute be so demanding?

And just when I think I can resist the siren call of his pitiful wails, he begins to pace. Oh, the pacing! It's like he's preparing for a marathon, darting back and forth like a contestant on a game show trying to win the grand prize. He'll circle the living room, then the kitchen, then back again, as if he's plotting a route to the nearest exit. I half-expect him to pull out a map and start marking the best spots for a quick bathroom break.

Finally, if I haven't caved by now, he resorts to the grand finale: the "I'm going to sit right by the door and stare at it until you feel so uncomfortable that you have no choice but to let me out" maneuver. It's a classic move, and it works every time. He'll sit there, his body language screaming urgency, as if the fate of the universe rests on his ability to sniff the neighbor's mailbox.

And then there's the moment of truth. I get up, fully aware that I've been outsmarted by a creature who thinks the world revolves around his bladder. I open the door, and he bolts outside like he's been released from a maximum-security prison. It's like watching a rocket launch. He's off, tail wagging, bounding into the yard like he's just discovered the meaning of life. Meanwhile, I'm left standing there, wondering how I got played by a dog who can't even spell "outside."

But you know what? As I watch him frolic in the grass, chasing after imaginary foes and rolling around like a deranged tumbleweed, I can't help but smile. Maybe he's not just begging to go outside; maybe he's reminding me that life is about those little moments of joy, even if it takes a little negotiation to get there.

From Pool to Porcelain: The Mysterious Case of a Dog's Toilet Fixation

You know, there's something about a dog that just makes you question the very fabric of your reality. I mean, take my dog, for example. Sweet little furball of joy and chaos wrapped in a coat of golden fluff. I love him dearly, but let's just say he has some... peculiar habits. Like, for instance, his absolute obsession with the toilet. Yes, the toilet. That porcelain throne we humans revere as a place of privacy and contemplation. To him, it's a five-star buffet.

Now, I've caught him in the act more times than I can count. I'll be minding my business, perhaps scrolling through social media or trying to find that elusive perfect avocado toast recipe, when suddenly, I hear it: the unmistakable slurping sound that could only mean one thing. I rush to the bathroom, and there he is, my dog, tongue deep in the bowl, living his best life. It's like he's discovered the Holy Grail of hydration, and I'm left standing there, mouth agape, wondering how this became my reality.

I mean, who needs a fancy water bowl when you have a toilet? Dogs have the uncanny ability to find the most disgusting things on the planet and treat them like they're gourmet delicacies. I can't help but imagine the thought process behind it. "Hmm, water bowl? Nah. Too basic. But wait! What's that shiny white thing in the corner? It's got a lid, but I can definitely work with that." And then, there he is, living out his wildest dreams, tongue swirling around in the bowl like it's the most refreshing ocean in the world.

And let's not even talk about the logistics of it. I mean, how does he even get in there? It's like he's part acrobat, part magician. One minute, he's lounging on the couch, and the next, he's somehow managed to leap over the bathroom threshold, defying all laws of physics to get to that bowl. It's like watching a nature documentary where the narrator is whispering about the majestic creature in its natural habitat, except the creature is my dog, and the habitat is a bathroom that I just cleaned.

I've tried everything to deter him. I've bought fancy water bowls that promise to be "just like the real thing." I've placed them strategically around the house, hoping he'll take the hint. But no, my dog looks at them like they're a sad imitation of the real deal. "What is this? A shallow puddle? Where's the excitement? Where's the mystery?" He snubs them with the same disdain I reserve for lukewarm coffee.

And it's not just the act of drinking from the toilet; it's the aftermath that really gets me. There's something about a dog that's just had the time of his life with his head in the toilet that is both hilarious and horrifying. He emerges, tail wagging, looking like he just won the lottery. And I'm left standing there, trying to reconcile the image of my beloved pet with the knowledge that he's just been mouth-deep in a bowl that's seen things—things I don't even want to think about.

"Hey buddy, how about a nice refreshing bowl of clean water?" I'll suggest, desperately trying to steer him away from his newfound obsession. But he looks at me like I'm trying to serve him broccoli for dessert. "Nah, Mom. This is the good stuff."

And honestly, I can't help but laugh. Because in that moment, I realize that this is the essence of dog life. They don't care about societal norms or hygiene. They live for the thrill, the adventure, the absolute absurdity of sticking their heads in a toilet. And honestly, who could blame them? If I had the choice between a mundane glass of water and the wild unknown of a toilet bowl, I might just be tempted to join them.

From "The REAL Cat Owner's Survival Guide"

But Is It Butt-Worthy?

You know, I've been thinking a lot about the mysteries of life lately, and one of the greatest enigmas I've encountered is the behavior of cats. I mean, have you ever noticed how a cat will just casually saunter up to you, look you dead in the eye, and then present its backside like it's the most natural thing in the world? It's like they're saying, "Hey, human! Want to see my finest asset?" I can't help but wonder what's going through their little feline minds.

Picture this: you're sitting on the couch, minding your own business, perhaps scrolling through your phone or watching a show, when suddenly—BAM! Your cat decides it's time for a butt presentation. It's as if they've been practicing this move, perfecting the angle, the posture, the tail lift. It's a full-on performance, and you're the captive audience. I swear, if there were a cat Olympics, this would be a gold medal event.

Honestly, it's a bold move. I mean, if I were to walk up to someone and show them my behind, I'd probably get slapped with a restraining order. But cats? They do it with such confidence, as if they're saying, "Look at me! I'm fabulous!" And what's even more perplexing is that this isn't just a one-time thing. No, no, no. This is a ritual. They come back for encore performances. It's like they're trying to start a trend. "Hey, everyone! Butt showing is the new thing! Get on board!"

And let's talk about the timing. Why do they choose the most inappropriate moments to do this? You could be in the middle of an important Zoom call, and there it is—Mr. Whiskers, presenting his rear end to the camera like he's auditioning for a reality show. "Yes, I know you're trying to look professional, but have you seen my tail? It's magnificent!" You can almost hear the collective gasp of your coworkers. I mean, who needs a cat filter when you have an actual cat butt photobombing your meeting?

Then there's the smell factor. Oh, the smell factor. I don't know if they're aware of their own hygiene or if they just assume we'll overlook the less-than-pleasant aroma wafting from their behinds. It's like they think, "Sure, I rolled in something unspeakable yesterday, but look at this cute little wiggle!" I'm left standing there, torn between admiration for their audacity and a desperate need to open a window.

What's even funnier is the way they react after the presentation. They turn around, look at you, and then strut away as if they've just delivered the punchline of the century. "Did you see that? Did you see what I just did? You're welcome!" Meanwhile, I'm sitting there, trying to process what just happened, questioning my life choices and wondering if I should be flattered or offended.

And let's not forget the sheer absurdity of it all. Here we are, in a world filled with serious issues and existential dread, and yet, the highlight of my day is my cat's butt. It's a reminder that sometimes, life doesn't need to be taken so seriously. Sometimes, it's okay to just laugh at the ridiculousness of it all.

So, here's to our furry companions and their unapologetic butt presentations. May we all learn a thing or two from them—like how to embrace our quirks, how to strut our stuff with confidence, and, most importantly, how to find joy in the simple things. And if that means putting our behinds on display every now and then, well, maybe that's not such a bad thing after all.

https://app.videogen.io/view/brdsur

Cat Litter: Diggin' And A-Scratchin'

You ever watch a cat use a litter box? It's like observing a tiny, furry archaeologist at work, digging through layers of history with the utmost seriousness. I mean, you'd think they were unearthing some ancient treasure rather than just doing their business. There's this whole ritual involved, a performance that would make even the most seasoned Broadway actor jealous. First, the cat approaches the litter box with an air of importance, tail held high like a flag of sovereignty. You can almost hear the dramatic music playing in the background, setting the stage for what's about to unfold.

Now, here's where the magic happens. The cat hops in, and you can see the gears turning in its little brain. It squats down, and you think, "Okay, this is it. This is the moment." And then—oh, the suspense!—the cat does its thing. But it's not just any ordinary business; it's a masterpiece of nature. The sound is barely audible, almost like a whisper, as if the cat is trying to keep this whole affair a secret from the world. "Shh, don't tell anyone," it seems to say, "I'm a dignified creature, and this is just between us."

Once the deed is done, the real show begins. The cat leaps up, and for a brief moment, it surveys its work, as if assessing the quality of the output. You can almost see the pride radiating from it. "Look at what I've created!" it seems to think. But wait, the best part is yet to come. With a determined look, the cat dives back into the litter box, armed with its tiny paws, ready to bury the evidence. It's like watching a master sculptor at work, carefully crafting a mound of litter over its masterpiece. The way it digs and scratches, you'd think it was trying to unearth buried treasure rather than cover up what could only be described as a biological necessity.

And here's the kicker: the cat is so intense about this process. It's as if it believes that if it doesn't cover it up perfectly, the world will somehow come crashing down. "What if someone finds out?" it seems to ponder, frantically pawing at the litter. "What if the neighbors see? I can't let the dogs down the street know my secrets!" The urgency is palpable, and you can't help but chuckle at the sheer absurdity of it all. You've got this majestic creature, a predator that could take down a bird in a single leap, reduced to a paranoid little fluffball worried about its bathroom habits.

Now, let's talk about the technique. There's an art to burying poop, and cats have perfected it over millennia. They kick up litter like they're trying to start a sandstorm. It's not just a gentle pat here and there; oh no, this is full-on excavation. You can practically hear them saying, "If I don't bury this deep enough, I might as well have left it out in the open for everyone to see!" And they really get into it—spinning around, flinging litter everywhere, as if they're in the midst of a catnip-fueled frenzy. You'd think they were conducting a symphony, each paw movement a note in a grand composition.

Finally, after what feels like an eternity of digging, the cat stands back, surveying its work with the satisfaction of an artist unveiling a masterpiece. "Behold, my work of art!" it seems to declare, tail flicking with pride. And then, as if on cue, it struts out of the litter box like it just conquered a mountain, leaving behind a perfectly covered pile that would make any archaeologist weep with joy. It's a moment of triumph, a victory in the daily grind of cat life.

And as I watch this whole spectacle unfold, I can't help but think: if only we humans could approach our own responsibilities with half the dedication and flair that a cat shows in burying its poop.

https://app.videogen.io/view/snollc

Dispatch, We Have The Zoomies In Progress

You know, there's something utterly ridiculous about the phenomenon we've all come to know and love as "the zoomies." It's that magical moment when your otherwise dignified feline transforms into a furry tornado, a furry embodiment of chaos. One minute, they're curled up on the couch, looking like a fluffy little potato, and the next, they're hurtling through the house like a miniature rocket. You'd think they were possessed by some hyperactive spirit, but no, it's just a cat being a cat.

I mean, let's talk about the sheer absurdity of it all. One moment, they're in deep hibernation, dreaming of world domination or perhaps plotting to overthrow the dog next door, and the next, they're leaping off the furniture like an Olympic gymnast. You can practically hear the dramatic music playing in the background as they launch themselves off the couch, their little paws barely touching the ground as they become a blur of fur and enthusiasm. It's like someone hit the fast-forward button on their life, and they've suddenly decided that the living room is their personal racetrack.

And let's not forget the sound effects. Oh, the sound effects! You'd think they were training for the feline version of the Indy 500. The pitter-patter of their paws echoes through the house like a stampede of tiny elephants. It's a cacophony that could wake the dead, and yet, there's something almost endearing about it. You can't help but chuckle as they zoom past you, their eyes wide and wild, as if they've just discovered a hidden stash of catnip. In that moment, they're not just a pet; they're an athlete in the prime of their career, a furry little superstar on a quest for glory.

But where exactly are they racing to? That's the million-dollar question. Is there a finish line somewhere in the kitchen? Are they trying to catch the elusive red dot of the laser pointer that's taunted them for years? Or maybe they're just trying to assert their dominance over the living room rug, claiming it as their territory with every chaotic leap. It's as if they've suddenly decided that the house is their playground, and they're the reigning champion of the zoomies.

And then, just as suddenly as it began, it stops. One moment, you're witnessing a feline frenzy, and the next, they come to a screeching halt, panting as if they just completed a marathon. They look around, bewildered, as if they've just woken up from a dream and are trying to make sense of the chaos they've created. It's like they're thinking, "What just happened? Did I really just leap off the bookshelf? Where's my dignity?"

And here's the kicker: you can't help but laugh. You're standing there, trying to contain your amusement, but it's impossible. There's something inherently funny about a creature that's supposed to be all about grace and poise suddenly losing their marbles. It's a reminder that even the most refined beings can have their moments of sheer silliness.

You start to wonder if they're secretly judging you for your lack of enthusiasm. "Look at me, human! I can fly! Why aren't you joining me?" And you're left there, holding your coffee, half-amused and half-concerned about the state of your furniture.

So, the next time your cat gets the zoomies, just sit back and enjoy the show. Embrace the chaos. After all, it's not every day you get to witness a furry whirlwind of energy tearing through your home. It's a reminder that life is too short to take too seriously, and sometimes, you just need to let loose and run wild—preferably with a little more grace than a cat, but hey, we can't all be furry tornadoes.

https://app.videogen.io/view/nwtxgd

Rub My Belly, Take Your Chances

You know, there's something utterly ridiculous about the way cats behave, particularly when they decide to roll over and present their belly to you like it's some kind of sacred offering. It's as if they're saying, "Behold! The soft underbelly of the mighty feline!" But let's be honest here; it's less of a display of trust and more of a challenge. It's like they're daring you to engage in a game of "Will you or won't you?" with the stakes being your own dignity and a possible trip to the emergency room.

I mean, picture this: you're sitting there, minding your own business, maybe scrolling through your phone, when suddenly, your cat—let's call him Mr. Whiskers—decides it's time to flaunt his fluff. He rolls over with the grace of a drunken ballerina, legs splayed out like he's auditioning for a role in a circus. And there it is, the belly, the holy grail of cat anatomy, gleaming with the promise of softness and warmth. You can't help but think, "Oh, how cute!" But then, a little voice in the back of your head whispers, "Danger, Will Robinson! Danger!"

Now, if you're a cat person, you know the rules. You've read the manuals, watched the YouTube videos, and maybe even consulted a feline psychologist. You know that a cat's belly is not just a belly; it's a no-fly zone, a forbidden territory. It's like the cat version of Area 51. You can look, but you cannot touch. Touching is an invitation for chaos, a summons for claws and teeth to spring into action like they've been training for this moment their entire lives. But there's Mr. Whiskers, sprawled out like he's auditioning for a catnip commercial, and you're torn between the urge to rub that fluffy belly and the fear of losing a finger in the process.

So, what do you do? You sit there, staring at him, contemplating life choices. You think about how you've fed him, cleaned his litter box, and provided endless entertainment with that laser pointer. Surely, you've earned the right to give that belly a gentle scratch, right? But as you stretch your hand out, you can almost hear the ominous music playing in the background, warning you of the impending doom. It's like a scene from a horror movie: the unsuspecting hero reaches for the belly, and the audience collectively gasps, knowing full well what's about to happen.

And then, the moment of truth arrives. You touch the belly, and for a fleeting second, it feels like you've won the lottery. Mr. Whiskers purrs, and your heart swells with pride. You're the chosen one! But just as quickly, the mood shifts. His eyes narrow, and suddenly, you're on the receiving end of a furry tornado. Claws are out, and you're left wondering if you should have just settled for a simple head scratch instead.

But let's not forget the sheer audacity of these creatures. They know exactly what they're doing. It's like they've concocted a master plan to keep us on our toes, to remind us who really runs the house. They roll over, flashing that belly, and we fall for it every single time. We're like moths to a flame, helplessly drawn in, only to get burned.

So, the next time you find yourself in the presence of a belly-flopping cat, remember: it's not just a display of affection; it's a test of your resolve, a challenge to your sanity. And as you weigh your options, just know that whatever you decide, you're in for a wild ride. Because in the world of cats, nothing is ever as simple as it seems.

https://app.videogen.io/view/zldnvc

Also by Michael Pollick